Dr Christopher McNall is a barrister, mediator and arbitrator. He specialises in disputes about farms and farming (and especially disputes about tenancies under the Agricultural Holdings Act 1986), taxation (especially of agricultural land, buildings and other assets), proprietary estoppel, and Inheritance Act claims. He has advised and appeared in many leading agricultural and tax cases in courts, tribunals and arbitrations throughout the UK. He holds a variety of fee-paid judicial offices, including Chairperson (Principal Judge) of the Agricultural Land Tribunal for Wales / Tribiwnlys Tir Amaethyddol Cymru. He is also a member of the Agricultural Law Association's Dispute Resolution Service and a Fellow of the Agricultural Law Association. The views expressed in this book are entirely his personal views.

A Practical Guide to the Law of Agricultural Tenancies in England and Wales

Third Edition

A Practical Guide to the Law of Agricultural Tenancies in England and Wales

Third Edition

Christopher McNall
MA (Oxon) DPhil (Oxon) FRSA FALA
Barrister, 18 St John Street Chambers, Manchester

Law Brief Publishing

Published 2026 by Law Brief Publishing, an imprint of Law Brief Publishing Ltd
30 The Parks
Minehead
Somerset
TA24 8BT

www.lawbriefpublishing.com

Paperback: 978-1-918241-36-5

To S and F

PREFACE

This book, which has now reached its third edition, is an introduction to the law of agricultural tenancies in England and Wales, written principally for the non-specialist legal practitioner and non-legal professionals.[1] Given its brevity, it cannot aim to be even remotely comprehensive, nor to be any substitute for the magisterial (but lengthy) specialist practitioners' works.[2] But, even though this book is only introductory, in reading it you are taking a worthwhile step in developing your knowledge of this interesting and challenging field.

This book aims to be both useful and value for money. It will guide you round some of the main landmarks of the law of agricultural tenancies, especially those held under the Agricultural Holdings Act 1986 ('the 1986 Act'). Its approach is practical and not academic. Along the way, I shall point out some of the biggest pitfalls to avoid. All this, from beginning to end, should take no more than two or three uninterrupted hours of your time.

If this book does its job, it will give you enough knowledge to be able to identify an agricultural tenancy problem when you see one (not always easy), and, having done so, to know that the problem may have to be dealt with using special tools, rather than by adopting and adapting knowledge from other forms of commercial land-holding (such as business tenancies under Part II of the Landlord and Tenant Act 1954). After you have read it, you should still be able to dip into

---

1 I do not deal with the law of agricultural tenancies in Scotland. For those, see Lord Gill's Agricultural Tenancies. For the law of Northern Ireland, and the special forms of land use there (such as conacre) see (for example) J C W Wylie's Irish Land Law.

2 See the Appendix.

this book as and when needed to give you a quick steer as to the sort of questions you should be asking of your client (and yourself) or to find out where to look for more detailed guidance.

In this edition, as well as updating the text of the second edition and setting out some further thoughts, I have included some entirely new material, including on the important amendments to the 1986 Act made by the Agriculture Act 2020, but now (after several years' waiting) in force, and in particular the abolition of the commercial occupation test, and the substantial revisions to the suitability test. I have also taken the opportunity to refer to some of the interesting and important court and tribunal decisions about the 1986 Act which have emerged in the last few years.

The recognition of agricultural law as a distinct field of expertise owes much to Nigel Davis, Graham Smith, Eleanor Pinfold, and Geoff Whittaker, who created and led the Agricultural Law Association's Fellowship programme – a potent cross-disciplinary mix of law, tax, succession planning – now well into its second decade, and continuing to prosper under the direction of Mike Holland and Dr Nerys Llewellyn-Jones. Practitioners are encouraged to join the ALA, which, as well as running courses, publishes a Bulletin and holds an annual dinner.

I came to agricultural law entirely by chance. When still a pupil barrister, now over 20 years ago, I was instructed to represent a dairy farmer in a dispute about the death of his herd after eating contaminated feed. Since then, I have been very fortunate in continuing to work alongside, and to learn from, many skilled fellow practitioners. Special mention goes to Oliver Wilson (who sent me those first instructions) and Liz Power at Nigel Davis Solicitors, Kevin Kennedy at Burges Salmon, Maddie Dunn (formerly of Burges Salmon, now at Charles Russell Speechlys), Tim Wolley at Bowcock and Pursaill, and Tim Russ (now elevated to the District Bench, formerly at Roythornes).

This book aims to state the law of England and Wales as at 1 April 2026.

Christopher McNall
The Feast of St Expeditus, 2026

CONTENTS

Chapter One	Introduction	1
Chapter Two	The Two Types of Agricultural Tenancies	7
Chapter Three	Agricultural Holdings Act 1986	17
Chapter Four	Succession to a 1986 Act Tenancy	49
Chapter Five	Dispute Resolution	61
Appendix A	Suggested Further Reading	67
Appendix B	Useful Addresses and Contact Details	69

CHAPTER ONE

INTRODUCTION

A significant majority of the land in England and Wales[1] is agricultural land – that is to say, is pasture or land used for the production of crops.[2]

Much of that agricultural land is tenanted. In 2025, about half the farms in England were wholly or partly tenanted. Across England and Wales, tenanted farms vary from massive moorland sprawls[3] to tiny arable patches – with everything in between. The average farm size in England is about 215 acres[4] (equivalent to about 200 football pitches).

This book concentrates on two aspects of the law of agricultural tenancies which are regularly encountered but sometimes imperfectly understood: the recovery of possession of agricultural holdings under the Agricultural Holdings 1986 Act (**'the 1986 Act'**) and the making

---

1 This book does not address the law in Scotland or in Northern Ireland.

2 The annual 'Farming Evidence Pack' produced by DEFRA and the Government Statistical Service is very useful. It can be found online. At the time of writing, the most recent update was October 2025.

3 The highest incidence of wholly tenanted farms in England (22% of farms) is in Northumberland. The lowest (12%) is Devon and Cornwall. Deep historical reasons lie behind each figure.

4 87 hectares (ha). 1 ha (= 100m x 100m = 10,000 m2) = about 2.47 acres. Hectares are metric. Acres are not. Traditionally, an acre (1/640th of a square mile) was the area which could be ploughed by one man in one day). If this book succeeds in conveying only one piece of information, remember the conversion from hectares to acres. It will definitely come in handy.

and opposition to succession applications to agricultural tenancies under that Act.[5]

Agricultural tenancy disputes abound, fuelled by two important trends. The first is that farmland continues to increase in value,[6] a long-term trend fuelled by advantageous tax treatment.[7] The second is that farming tenants are getting older. In 2025 (and continuing a long trend) about 2/3rds of agricultural farmholders (both tenants and owners) were aged 55 or older. The death or retirement of a 1986 Act tenant is (at least potentially) a succession event and so is capable of giving rise to dispute.[8]

---

5 With some exceptions, tenancies first granted on or before 12 July 1984 carry succession rights. There are still lots of these tenancies around. 1984 is only 42 years ago. Someone who took a tenancy in June 1984 aged 21 has still not even reached the State pension age.

6 Available market figures suggest an increase of about 26% since 2020, with an average of about £8,250 an acre (= £20,300 a hectare). Applied to the average 87 ha holding, this is £1.77m, excluding the value of the farmhouse and agricultural buildings.

7 Capital Gains Tax roll-over relief allows farmers with profits from the sale of land for development to roll-over those profits into the purchase of farmland without paying CGT. Agricultural Property Relief has also made agricultural land and buildings very attractive to investors seeking to minimise the impact of Inheritance Tax on their estates. Only time will tell whether the imminent IHT changes effect the market for farmland.

8 The financial stakes leading a landlord to resist a succession application or to give a Notice to Quit when the opportunity arises can be enormous. If a 1986 AHT rent is about half of the rent otherwise available (eg compare about £180/acre (FBT) to £90/acre (AHT)), then 87 ha gives an annual opportunity cost / 'lost rent' to the landlord of £19,350. Factoring in up to two successions (say, 60 years) = £1.161m.

The Tribunal

Resolution of many 1986 Act disputes does not lie with judges in the court system, but instead lies in the parallel Tribunals system. In England, this is the Agricultural Lands and Drainage Division of the Property Chamber of the First-tier Tribunal. In Wales[9] it is the Agricultural Land Tribunal for Wales / Tribiwnlys Tir Amaethyddol Cymru. In this book, I shall refer to these as 'the Tribunal'.[10]

Neither Tribunal is a superior court of record, and so neither has the power formally to bind the Tribunal in any subsequent case. But the Tribunal is a specialist judge-led jurisdiction, and so its decisions (especially those dealing with wider points of principle or practice) may merit attention. The Welsh Tribunal publishes its decisions online.[11] The English Tribunal does not presently do so.

Although the 1986 Act applies both in England and Wales, the procedural rules which govern the work of the Tribunal in England (The Tribunal Procedure (First-tier Tribunal) (Property Chamber)

If the average farm (see above) is worth something like £2m, and the Open Market Value is diminished by (say) 50% on account of a 1986 Act tenancy, then the potential surrender value of the extant tenancy is up to £1m.

9 Because agricultural matters in Wales are devolved to the Wales Government. This gives rise not only to the separate devolved Wales tribunal, but also to different secondary legislation in England and Wales, for example, in relation to the 'Model Clauses': see below.

10 For addresses and other contact details, see the Appendix.

11 agriculturallandtribunal.gov.wales These are not available on bailii or other databases.

Rules 2013: SI 2013/1169) are not the same as those in Wales (The Agricultural Lands Tribunal (Rules) Order 2007: SI 2007/3105).

If you are involved with a Tribunal, make sure you are using the right rules. There are important differences. For example, appeals from each Tribunal lie to the Lands Chamber of the Upper Tribunal, but appeals from the Welsh Tribunal lie as of right, and without any need for permission; whereas appeals from the English Tribunal can be made only with permission and if raising an arguable error of law. The circumstances in which costs may be awarded are also different. In Wales, costs lie where conduct has been 'vexatious, frivolous, or oppressive'; arguably a higher test than the 'unreasonable conduct' threshold in England.[12]

Other important and regularly-encountered disputes in the context of the 1986 Act (such as the recovery of tenanted land for the purposes of development)[13] cannot be dealt with by the Tribunal. They must be referred to arbitration.

After reforms to the 1986 Act made by the Deregulation Act 2015, some sorts of disputes which previously could only be referred to

---

12 There are very few reported decisions on costs. In Carr v Evelyn (ALD/SE/S/2016/006, April 2020) the Tribunal made a costs order against a party who had engaged an expert who the Tribunal found 'was demonstrably partisan' and not truly independent. In Jones v Steyer (ALT 19/2021, August 2025) the Tribunal ordered that a landlord pay the tenant's costs where the landlord had withdrawn its application for a certificate of bad husbandry part way through the hearing. The landlord's conduct was found to have been 'oppressive'.

13 Special Case 'B'

arbitration can now be referred (but only if the parties agree) to 'Third Party Determination' (TPD).[14]

Arbitrations in relation to the 1986 Act are usually conducted by a single arbitrator nominated (at the election of the person seeking the appointment) either by the President of RICS (ie, a surveyor from its Dispute Resolution Service), the Chairperson of the Agricultural Law Association (who will nominate a member of the ALA's Dispute Resolution Panel), or the Chairperson of the Central Association of Agricultural Valuers.

The default position is that arbitrations, regardless of the identity or profession of the arbitrator, are conducted under the terms of the Arbitration Act 1996.

In contrast, the procedure under which a 'Third Party Determination' is to be conducted is not subject to the 1996 Arbitration Act. It seems that the parties are free to agree any procedure they want.[15]

14 See the Chapter on Dispute Resolution

15 My only experience of TPD is that the parties wanted the Arbitration Act 1996 to apply. That was convenient, but not required.

CHAPTER TWO

THE TWO TYPES OF AGRICULTURAL TENANCIES

Two main Acts of Parliament apply to tenanted agricultural land in England and Wales. The statutes are mutually exclusive. Any individual parcel of tenanted land is held under the terms of one statute, or the other. It cannot be held under both.

The first is the Agricultural Holdings Act 1986 (**'the 1986 Act'**). Tenancies under the 1986 Act are often called 'AHTs' ('Agricultural Holding Tenancies') or '86 Act tenancies'.

The 1986 Act is a consolidating Act, and replaces – albeit in largely identical terms – the Agricultural Holdings Act 1948 (**'the 1948 Act'**). As such, reported decisions about the meaning and effect of the 1948 Act can and often are applied to disputes about the same provision in the 1986 Act. Tenancies granted as early as 1948 (but which are now subject to the 1986 Act) do still exist.[16]

---

16 Although tenants of this vintage are now few and far between (a 21-year old in 1948 would now be 99). More commonly, one encounters AHTs granted to companies (ie, legal persons), often as a form of planning to obtain reliefs from Inheritance Tax and its predecessor taxes. So long as a company keeps up its filing requirements with Companies House, it does not 'die'. If you encounter this sort of scenario, seek professional advice from an accountant as to whether this antiquated tax planning is still going to work (it may not) or whether tinkering with it now will bring about adverse tax consequences (it may).

1986 Act tenancies are not only common but give rise to a host of challenging technical issues.

The second statute is the Agricultural Tenancies Act 1995 (**'the 1995 Act'**). Tenancies under the 1995 Act are often called 'FBTs' ('Farm Business Tenancies') or '95 Act tenancies'.

The 1986 Act is still in force. It was not repealed by the 1995 Act.

The 1986 Act and the 1995 Act are chalk and cheese. They could not really be more different in their content or operation.

The 1948 Act was part of the suite of socially progressive legislation introduced by the post-World War 2 Labour government which also created the NHS and the State education system. The 1948 Act was designed to improve the fairly miserable lot of tenant farmers, as a gesture of gratitude for keeping the country fed during the war.[17]

The 1986 Act (and the 1948 Act before it) is definitely 'tenant friendly', not least in conferring what often effectively amounts to lifelong security of tenure.

The 1948 Act, and the 1986 Act, are each self-contained, very detailed, statutory 'Codes'. This means that the answer to most questions about 1986 Act tenancies is to be found in the precise wording of the 1986 Act. There is some room, but not much, for the common law to intrude.[18]

---

17 See the discussion on agricultural security in Mark Wonnacott, The History of the Law of Landlord and Tenant in England and Wales (2012), pp 159 and following.

18 An example: The notice period is to be found in the statute, but the rules about the validity of the notice in terms of accuracy etc are

Tenancies under the 1995 Act are very different to 1986 Act tenancies. The 1995 Act, and FBTs created under it, are the product of libertarian ideas of freedom of contract and also the idea that landowners would be encouraged to let out land to those entering the farming profession if able to do so without triggering the security of tenure consequences of the 1986 Act.

As to freedom of contract, as long as certain overarching conditions are met,[19] the 1995 Act leaves landlords and tenants to their own devices to strike whatever deal they want to, and the terms of their FBT embody that individual deal.

Unlike the 1986 Act, the 1995 Act tenant never enjoys any security of tenure for longer than the term granted.[20] The 1995 Act is not really a detailed statutory code at all. It simply establishes some fairly basic ground rules. Beyond that, the parties are on their own.

This means that many problems which arise in relation to FBTs are best solved by looking to the tenancy agreement, and what it says. There are 'off-the-peg' standard form FBTs (for example, from the Royal Institute of Chartered Surveyors and the Country Landowners Association). These are often very lengthy and detailed, making sophisticated provision for all sorts of contingencies. However,

---

common law rules.

19 A valid FBT can only exist if the 'business condition' in section 1 of the 1995 Act is met (land farmed for the purpose of a trade or business), as well as either the 'agriculture condition' (the character of the tenancy is primarily or wholly agricultural) or the 'notice condition' (on or before the start of the tenancy, the parties gave each other written notice that the tenancy was to be an FBT): see, further, below.

20 An FBT for a fixed term of up to 2 years does not need to be terminated by notice.

because no tenancy agreement can ever deal with every possible eventuality, or be completely comprehensive, if you have an FBT problem and the answer is not in the tenancy agreement, then you are in the undesirable position of having to imply terms (if you can) for example by way of necessity or business efficacy.[21] Going to court to seek to imply a term into an FBT is not the most enticing prospect.

Which Act applies?

The best way of telling which Act applies is to look at the date on which the tenancy was first granted. If it was first granted on or after **1 September 1995** (the date on which the 1995 Act came into force) it cannot (except in certain unusual circumstances – see below) be a tenancy under the 1986 Act.

1 September 1995. Remember the date!

If you want to stop reading here, you have already justified your financial outlay in this book.

If a tenancy was first granted on or after 2 September 1995, then you are probably in 1995 Act territory and so probably do not need to trouble yourself with the intricacies of the 1986 Act.

Note the 'probablies'. There are some wrinkles. It is possible for a tenancy to be an AHT even if granted (NB, not first granted) today.

21 See (for example) the Supreme Court's decision in *Marks and Spencer plc v BNP Paribas* [2015] UKSC 72.

A good example of this would be a 1986 Act succession tenancy granted today[22] or obtained by virtue of a direction of the Tribunal.[23]

1995 Act Tenancies / FBTs

Tenancies under the Agricultural Tenancies Act 1995 are Farm Business Tenancies ('FBTs') but are often known just as '95 Act' tenancies.

FBTs differ from 1986 Act tenancies in a number of very important ways. An FBT gives no security of tenure beyond that provided for in the tenancy agreement. An FBT does not create or give rise to any succession rights.

In order to be an FBT, the tenancy must meet certain statutory conditions. These are the 'Business Condition' and either the 'Agriculture Condition' or the 'Notice Condition'.

The 'Business Condition' is that all or part of the land is farmed for the purposes of a trade or business at the beginning of the tenancy, and some part remains so used at all times. The 1995 Act does not define 'farming'. Farming may or may not be the same as 'used for agriculture'.

22 See section 4(1)(d) of the 1995 Act which permits the post 1 September 1995 creation of a 1986 Act tenancy where it 'is granted on an agreed succession by a written contract of tenancy indicating (in whatever terms) that Part IV of the 1986 Act is to apply in relation to the tenancy'.

23 ATA 1995 Section 4(1)(b). Sections 4(1)(a)-(g) set out the full list of exceptions. On occasion, it can be difficult to work out whether these apply. Seek specialist advice.

The 'Agriculture Condition' is that, having regard to the terms of the tenancy, the use of the land, the nature of any commercial activities carried out on it, and any other relevant circumstances, the nature of the tenancy is wholly or primarily agricultural.

The 'Notice Condition' is that the parties have served on each other, at the commencement of the tenancy, written notices specifying that the tenancy shall remain an FBT even if the nature of the use of the land ceases, at some later date, to be primarily agricultural.

The Agricultural and Notice Conditions are designed to address different scenarios. The Agricultural Condition is suitable where, at the time the tenancy is granted, no substantial diversification from agricultural user is anticipated. Where the Notice Condition is met, the tenancy granted remains an FBT, even if the tenant changes the nature of their activity on the land from agriculture to something else. The Notice Condition therefore protects the landlord from an FBT 'changing code' because of a diversification into non-agricultural use which otherwise is capable (at least potentially) of turning the FBT into a business tenancy under the Landlord and Tenant Act 1954. That would be undesirable for a landlord because the 1954 Act could end up conferring much greater security of tenure on the tenant than an FBT. For that very reason, in practice, the Notice Condition is almost universally complied with by prudent landlords.

Any tenancy of agricultural land first granted on or after 1st September 1995 which meets the statutory conditions for an FBT will be (and, if the Notice Condition is met, will *remain*) an FBT (and not a 1986 Act tenancy) unless it falls within one of the exceptions set out in section 4 of the 1995 Act.

The main section 4 exceptions are (i) succession tenancies (whether on the tenant's death or retirement) granted by the Tribunal under the 1986 Act; (ii) tenancies granted in writing on an agreed succession with the tenancy agreement indicating that the 1986 Act is to apply; and (iii) tenancies granted to an existing tenant over the whole or substantially the whole of land already comprised in the holding, already held under a tenancy in relation to which the 1986 Act applied, and containing a clear statement that the 1986 Act is to apply to them.

It is clear that it is made (deliberately) difficult to (first) create a 1986 Act tenancy today. For better or worse, this significantly reduces the chance of accidentally creating one.

But there is a parallel problem, which is losing rights under the 1986 Act, without realising it, when things are done which have the effect of bringing about an implied surrender and regrant (surrender by operation of law) which can 'use up' a succession. Examples include adding a tenant to the tenancy, or adding land to the tenancy.

1995 Act Tenancies granted for a term of two years or less expire automatically, by effluxion of time: AHA 1995 section 5.

1995 Act Tenancies for more than 2 years require service of a written notice (expiring on the term date) at least 12 months before the term date. There is no prescribed form of notice. If the FBT is granted as a fixed term of more than two years, then it can only be brought to an end by such a notice to quit. If no notice to quit is given, then the FBT will continue as a periodic tenancy (from year to year) until terminated by at least 12 months' notice expiring on an anniversary of the term date.

1986 Act tenancies

I have already drawn attention to the importance of 1 September 1995. Any tenancy first granted before then cannot possibly be an FBT.

The second very important date to remember is **12 July 1984.** Any 1986 Act tenancy first granted before **12 July 1984** will be a 1986 Act tenancy which will, by default,[24] carry succession rights.

Any 1986 Act tenancy first granted between 12 July 1984 and 31 August 1995 will be governed by the 1986 Act, but with some watering down. These tenancies are secure for the original tenant, but generally do not carry any succession rights.

For those tenancies which have them, the existence of succession rights does not mean that there will actually be a succession. 'Succession rights' simply mean that an 'eligible' and 'suitable' (each as defined) aspirant successor, on the death or retirement of the tenant, may (if the landlord agrees) be granted a succession tenancy[25] or (if the landlord does not agree) may apply to the Tribunal for a succession tenancy.

The succession process (ie the vesting of an existing tenancy in a successor tenant) can happen up to twice – from the original tenant to first successor (succession 1) and from the first successor to the second successor (succession 2).

---

24 That is to say, regardless of whether a written tenancy agreement makes any reference to them.

25 Which, even though granted after 1 September 1995, will not be an FBT but will be an AHA, because one of the exceptions created by section 4 of the 1995 Act.

The 1986 Act sets out statutory tests to determine whether someone is 'eligible' and 'suitable'.

Bearing in mind that the original tenant themselves may well enjoy lifelong security of tenure, then extending that prospect not only to successor one but also, in due course, to successor two could potentially mean a tenancy lasting for three lifetimes – perhaps well over a century. I have encountered tenancies granted in the 1950s or 1960s where the tenancy (then a 1948 Act tenancy, now a 1986 Act tenancy) is still in the hands of the original (natural person) tenant.

Hence, the economic impact of a 1986 Act tenancy with succession rights can be dramatic. It is generally understood that the rent of an AHT carrying succession rights is less than the rent for an FBT, and that the presence of an AHT exerts a depressing effect on Open Market Value (OMV). In financial terms, over three generations, and decades, this can be significant.[26]

26 See my rough-and-ready calculation above. The obvious corollary is that an aspirant successor could, if so minded, seek to ransom the landlord, who might prefer to buy off a succession, in exchange for a long FBT (eg, 25 years, giving the tenant a sufficiently long interest to raise capital for investment), rather than risk the Tribunal directing a succession tenancy (especially if it is a first succession with a prospective second successor already on the horizon).

CHAPTER THREE

AGRICULTURAL HOLDINGS ACT 1986

The statutory requirements

There are three statutory requirements for a 1986 Act tenancy.

Firstly, there has to be *'a contract of tenancy'*: section 1(1). In many cases this is easy to answer because the tenancy agreement is in writing (frequently using standard forms such as those provided by the Estates Gazette). But the 1986 Act does not require an AHT to be made by a deed, or even to be in writing. Many AHTs are annual tenancies, and as such (being tenancies for less than a term of three years) are exempt from the usual formality requirements for leases: see Law of Property Act 1925 section 54(2).

Valid AHTs can be – and often are – created orally (but remember – happening on or before 1 September 1995), just so long as the usual requirements for a binding contract are met: (i) an intention to create legal relations (family arrangements and 'gentlemen's agreements' may fail to satisfy this requirement); (ii) offer and matching acceptance; and (iii) consideration. It is also possible – although quite unusual – for a tenancy (which is just a type of contract) to be created by conduct. That would call for the consensual assumption of exclusive possession for agricultural purposes, coupled with the payment and receipt of rent or consideration of some kind.

Where a tenancy is oral, or concluded by conduct, or even in writing, the 1986 Act contains a mechanism for the implication of an extensive series of terms: see the discussion below about the 'Model Clauses' and section 7.

Section 2 tenancies

Section 2 of the 1986 Act can sometimes engage. This section embodies a sort of 'statutory magic' which converts certain non-gratuitous licences and other arrangements (whether in writing or not) which were in existence on 1 September 1995 into fully-fledged 1986 Act tenancies '*where the circumstances are such that if [the occupant's] interest were a tenancy from year to year he would in respect of that land be the tenant of an agricultural holding*'. Interests of this nature are sometimes known as 'section 2 tenancies'. They are valid AHTs, but do not carry succession rights because they are deemed to have first come into existence on 1 September 1995.

For section 2 to operate, there still needs to be (i) an intention to create legal relations, (ii) exclusive occupation (meaning, at least, exclusive occupation for agricultural purposes, bearing in mind that fields, unlike rooms, do not have doors and windows which can be locked); and (iii) some consideration, although the requisite consideration need not be monetary, but can be something of value, such as keeping the land in good heart (Mitton v Farrow [1986] 2 EGLR 1) or agreeing to reseed after harvest (Davies v Davies [2002] EWCA Civ 1791). There are exceptions to section 2. For example, it expressly does not operate to convert grazing or mowing agreements 'during some specified period of the year' into agricultural tenancies: section 2(3).

Difficult questions can arise as to whether (for example) a series of 11-month grazing licences, first starting before 1 September 1995, but where the occupant has in fact been in continuous occupation, have given rise to a section 2 tenancy.[27]

The second requirement for an agricultural tenancy is that the land has to be *'let for use as agricultural land'*: section 1(2).

The meaning of 'agriculture'

'*Agriculture*' includes:

> '*horticulture, fruit growing, seed growing, dairy farming and livestock breeding and keeping, the use of land as grazing land, meadow land, osier land, market gardens and nursery grounds, and use of land for woodlands where that use is ancillary to the farming of land for other agricultural purposes*': section 96(1)[28]

This is not an exhaustive definition. For example, it does not include the growing of wheat, which is undoubtedly agricultural activity within the proper meaning and effect of the 1986 Act.

> '*Livestock*' includes '*any creature kept for the production of food, wool, skins, or fur or for the purpose of its use in the*

27 Instances of long occupation where the occupant is hazy as to the precise date on which they first went into occupation, except that it was 'some time in the summer of 1995', call for particularly anxious scrutiny.

28 Recent statutes (eg the *Agriculture (Wales) Act 2023* section 51) have introduced new elements to the definition of 'agriculture' for their purposes: eg, the use of land for agroforesty, or maintaining land in a state that makes it suitable for agriculture – that is to say, not actually food production of any kind.

farming of land or the carrying on in relation to land of any agricultural activity'.

The courts have interpreted this as ruling out, from being AHTs, instances where the agricultural activity consists of things such as pheasant rearing for sport and some sorts of equine use.

Whether equestrian activity is a qualifying activity for an AHT can be a grey area. In cases like Rutherford v Maurer [1962] 1 QB 16, it has been held that tenanted land used for grazing (= an agricultural purpose) by horses (not = livestock) in connection with a livery business or riding school (= a business, but not an *agricultural* business) is an agricultural holding within the meaning of the 1986 Act. But there are other cases where equine use has not given rise to an AHA because the land is not being used as grazing land: seek specialist advice.

Use for a trade or business

The third statutory requirement is that the land used for agriculture must be *'so used for the purposes of a trade or business'*: section 1(4). Whether activity is a trade or business for this purpose can be a matter of fact and degree, especially when the business activity is quite modest (for example, the use of land to produce and sell a grass crop for an annual income of a few hundred pounds, or the keeping of a few hens to sell eggs to the local shop or at the gate) and/or is not conducted on conventional business principles (for example, where it is more akin to a hobby). Sometimes courts look to the so-called 'badges of trade'. There can be difficult cases – for example, use of land as a community free farm has been held not to have given rise to an AHA (Secretary of State for Transport v Jenkins (1997) 79 P&CR 118). Again, seek specialist advice.

The 'Model Clauses': section 7

Section 7 of the 1986 Act incorporates the so-called 'Model Clauses' into all AHTs, whether written or oral. The Model Clauses concern the maintenance, repair and insurance of fixed equipment. Fixed equipment includes any building or structure affixed to the land, and any works on, in, over or under land – for example, the farmhouse and farm buildings, water and drainage systems, and gas, electrical and safety detection systems.

The Model Clauses are incorporated '*except insofar as they would impose on one of the parties to an agreement in writing a liability which under the agreement is imposed on the other*'. This means that the liabilities contemplated by the Model Clauses will apply unless the parties have agreed, in writing, something different. They apply without modification to all oral tenancies.

The full text of the Model Clauses is to be found in The Agriculture (Model Clauses for Fixed Equipment) (England) Regulations 2015 SI 2015/950 (England only) and the Agriculture (Model Clauses for Fixed Equipment) (Wales) Regulations 2019 SI 2019/1279 (W 223) (Wales only). The Agriculture (Maintenance, Repair, and Insurance of Fixed Equipment) Regulations 1973 are now repealed in their entirety.

The English and Welsh Regulations are each extremely detailed codes which allocate liabilities for maintaining and repairing a whole range of fixed equipment either to the landlord or to the tenant. The Regulations also regulate the amounts which can be claimed.

So, if the agreement lacks detail, and you want to know who (for example) has to pay to fix the smoke detector system in the milking parlour, the Regulations should provide the answer.

Schedule 1: Matters for which provision should be made in written tenancy agreements

In addition to the Model Clauses incorporated by virtue of section 7, Schedule 1 of the 1986 Act sets out a list of nine '*Matters for which provision is to be made in written tenancy agreements*'.

Schedule 1 applies to all tenancy agreements, whether written or oral. Some of these nine matters are obvious (and one would expect to see them in any written agreement): such as 'the term or terms for which the holding or different parts of it is or are agreed to be let' and 'the rent reserved and the dates on which it is payable'.

The most important item on the Schedule 1 list regularly encountered in practice is Paragraph 9: 'a covenant by the tenant not to assign, sub-let or part with possession of the holding or any part of it without the landlord's consent in writing': see below.

If the tenancy agreement – whether written or oral – fails to make provision for one or more of the matters in Schedule 1, and if the landlord and tenant cannot agree what provision should be made, then section 6 of the 1986 Act gives a mechanism for resolution. This is a process which begins with the giving of a so-called 'section 6 notice', by either the landlord or the tenant, to the other, requesting that the other enter into an agreement in writing embodying all the terms of the tenancy and all the Schedule 1 matters, and, in default of which, that the matter be referred to arbitration or Third Party Determination.

So, Schedule 1 (unlike the Model Clauses) does not actually give an answer to *what* the clause should be – it just gives the mechanism for the arbitrator / TPD to decide what the clause should be.

Assignment of a 1986 Act tenancy

Even though a 1986 Act tenancy is capable of conferring, in reality, what can amount to lifelong security of tenure on the tenant, this is not absolute. In relation to pre-12 July 1984 AHTs, the landlord may resist any succession application made when the tenant dies or retires.

The obvious way for a natural person tenant to try to forestall this scenario is to assign whilst still alive.[29] Assignment by a natural person (who will eventually die) to a legal person such as a company (which, as long as it does what is needed to remain on the Register at Companies House, may live for ever) is one way of trying to keep the tenancy alive. Assignments by natural persons to limited companies are frequently encountered, but are not free from risk. It must be borne in mind that, if the assignee company is itself to be the tenant, and is itself to have the benefit of a 1986 Act tenancy, then the assignee company *itself* needs to continue to satisfy the statutory conditions for the existence of a valid AHA tenancy, including occupying the land itself for the purposes of a trade or business. Hence, 'dormant' or non-trading companies, or companies which undertake non-agricultural activity (such as a B&B; glamping; holiday lets; agro-tourism) may fail to satisfy section 1(4) of the 1986 Act, thereby losing the protection of the 1986 Act – an unintended and undesirable outcome.[30]

---

29 You cannot effectively assign an AHA by will because a will is an ambulatory document which takes effect only at the moment of death; at which self-same moment the testator's estate has already vested in their executors: an application of the nemo dat principle.

30 Non-agricultural use / diversification scenarios sometimes entice the well-heeled and ambitious landlord to bring a claim seeking a declaration that the tenancy is no longer within the 1986 Act. Although such claims are perhaps superficially attractive, remember that the only iron law of litigation is the law of unintended consequences.

Most written tenancy agreements contain an anti-assignment covenant. The covenant often implied into commercial leases (that is, leases under the Landlord and Tenant Act 1954) that the landlord cannot unreasonably withhold consent to assignment is not implied into tenancies of agricultural holdings. As such, assignment without consent in breach of an express anti-assignment covenant in the lease is a dangerous step to take. It risks being treated as an irremediable breach of the lease, materially prejudicing the landlord's reversion, and thereby potentially giving the landlord scope to bring a 'Case E' Notice to Quit.

Where the tenancy (whether oral or in writing) is silent as to whether the tenant can assign, then there is a possibility of assignment (because all tenants have the common law right to assign).

The possibility of assignment by the tenant of their interest to a legal person (or, perhaps, to a much younger natural person) presents a real hazard for the landlord otherwise hoping to recover possession on the tenant's death (where there are no succession rights), or to object to a succession application (where there are succession rights).

Section 6 notices

The 1986 Act throws a lifeline to the landlord of a tenancy without an express prohibition on assignment. Where the agreement (whether oral or written) fails to make any provision for the matter in Schedule 1 Paragraph 9 – namely 'a covenant by the tenant not to assign, sub-let or part with possession of the holding or any part of it without the landlord's consent in writing' – then the landlord can request (which need not be in writing, but which prudently should be) that the tenant enter into a written agreement '*embodying all the terms of the tenancy and containing provision for all of the said matters*', and, in the absence of such agreement, that the terms of the tenancy should be referred to arbitration or third party determination.

Once a section 6 notice has been given by a landlord, it carries the very important consequence of preventing the tenant from assigning, sub-letting or parting with possession, of the whole or any part, without the landlord's consent in writing, *'during the period while the determination of the terms of the tenancy is pending'*: section 6(5). This is often referred to as 'the statutory standstill'. Any such transaction is void.

The same does not apply where the section 6 notice is given by the tenant. That is to say, a tenant's notice does not impose a standstill on assignment.

Therefore, a sensible landlord who faces an occupant who is or who may be a 1986 Act tenant, where the tenancy is oral, or arises from conduct, or is in writing but does not contain any anti-assignment clause, should always give urgent consideration to the making of a section 6 request (ideally, by giving a written notice) so as to prevent any valid or effective assignment by the tenant.

Only the party making the original request can demand arbitration. However, the 1986 Act does not give any timescale within which an arbitrator should be appointed. This gives rise to an arguably unresolved legal question as to whether section 6 notices, if not consummated by the appointment of an arbitrator, expire automatically through effluxion of time (the failure to pursue the notice being treated as a sort of waiver). Well-informed opinion is divided on this point. Some landlords periodically issue new section 6 notices, all without prejudice to the force, meaning, effect, and validity of any previous section 6 notices, but nonetheless do not then go on to demand arbitration (which only the giver of the notice may do). This thereby imposes, in reality, a running embargo on assignment.

If there is an arbitration as to the matters under Schedule 1 then the arbitrator cannot rewrite the tenancy agreement ad lib. Her power is limited to specifying the existing terms of the tenancy, and making provision for the Schedule 1 matters only where it is 'reasonable and just' to do so.

Recovering possession of a 1986 Act tenancy: Types of Notices to Quit

1986 Act tenancies do not expire by effluxion of time. Even the tenant's death does not bring such a tenancy to an end, because the benefit of the tenancy vests in the tenant's personal representatives (if executors, this vesting happens at the moment of death; if administrators, it happens only on the grant of letters of administration).[31]

The recovery of possession of land held under a 1986 Act tenancy can be complex, difficult, and time-consuming. It is full of traps for the unwary.

A key feature of the 1986 Act is that the tenant's security of tenure is achieved in effect by the imposition of restrictions on landlords' notices to quit and the conditions which must apply for valid and effective notices to quit to be given.

The recovery of possession under the 1986 Act is mainly a 'notice-based' system. This means that even when the tenant is in clear breach of a statutory or contractual obligation (for instance, the obligation to pay rent as and when due) that breach, in and of itself, is not sufficient to allow the landlord to bring a Notice to Quit or to recover

31 This gives rise to the requirement in some cases for the landlord to give notice to the Official Solicitor.

possession. In most instances, the landlord must give a written notice of some kind. Under the 1986 Act, it is the giving of the right notice at the right time in the right way which entitles the landlord to recover possession – not the underlying breach itself.

There are two main kinds of notice to quit affecting AHTs, and they are governed by different rules.

The first is a 'general' notice to quit (sometimes called an 'unqualified' notice). A general notice does not need to give any reason for wishing to recover possession (although it may) but it must be valid at common law (i.e., it must be sufficiently clear, unambiguous and precise: see Mannai Investment v Eagle Star [1995] 1 WLR 1508).[32]

Usually (but not always) at least 12 months' notice (expiring on a term date)[33] is required, even if the tenancy agreement says that less than 12 months notice is needed: section 25(1).

32 In *OG Thomas Amaethyddiaeth Cyf v Turner* [2022] EWCA Civ 1444, the Court of Appeal held that a notice addressed to a natural person (Mr Thomas) who had some days earlier assigned the tenancy to a company of which he was sole director (OG Thomas A. Cyf) was not correctly addressed, could not be rescued by the application of *Mannai* principles, and was therefore invalid. However, had the notice been simply addressed to 'the tenant', without naming anyone, or (perhaps) had it used some other formulation, it could possibly have been valid.

33 Get the date right. It is very easy to get it wrong. This may depend on whether the tenancy runs 'from' a certain date, or begins 'on' a certain date. The sensible approach is to always use 'running words' in a Notice to Quit as well as a specific date: just in case.

The second kind of notice to quit is a 'Special Case' notice. That is a notice which seeks to rely on one of the 'Special Cases' set out in Schedule 3 of the 1986 Act.

Case A	Smallholding termination provisions
Case B	Non-agricultural use for which planning permission has been granted
Case C	The Tribunal has awarded a certificate of bad husbandry
Case D	Non-compliance with a Notice to Pay Rent or a Notice to Remedy a breach of the tenancy
Case E	The tenant has committed an irremediable breach which materially prejudices the landlord
Case F	Tenant is insolvent
Case G	Death of tenant
Case H	Ministry tenancy

If a Special Case notice is to be given, it is particularly important to pay close attention to the wording of the Special Case and to get the wording absolutely right. Always use a tried-and-tested precedent.[34]

There is no restriction on the type or number of notices to quit that a landlord can give at one time.[35] A landlord can give a general notice to quit alongside one (or more) Special Case notices. The giving of a Special Case notice under one Case does not preclude the giving of a Special Case notice under another Case. Notices are often given expressly without prejudice to the force, validity, meaning and effect of any other notices. 1986 Act notices can also be given expressly without prejudice to the contention that no 1986 Act tenancy in fact exists[36] (for example, if it is considered that the tenancy has already come to an end for some reason, or if the evidence supporting the existence of a 1986 Act tenancy at all is thin or non-existent).[37]

Bringing and challenging a 'general' Notice to Quit

A valid Notice to Quit ends the tenancy.

However, section 26(1) of the 1986 Act gives the tenant a crucial safeguard. Where a general notice to quit is given and "*not later than one month from the giving of the notice to quit the tenant serves on the*

34 There are many in the Appendices of the leading practitioners' works.

35 Regulated legal professionals must be careful that the giving of multiple notices is done in a way which is fair and transparent, and which does not lead to a tenant's confusion (especially where a tenant is old or vulnerable).

36 The so-called 'Grammer v Lane' basis.

37 For example, where there is doubt as to whether the occupant was first in occupation before or after 1 September 1995.

landlord a counter-notice in writing requiring that this subsection shall not apply to the notice to quit" then (subject to s 26(2)) the notice to quit shall not have effect unless, on an application by the landlord, the Tribunal consents to its operation.

For a tenant receiving a general notice to quit, **speed is of the essence!** In responding to a general notice to quit, the tenant's counter-notice must be served within one month from the giving of the notice to quit. This is a rigid and inflexible time limit. The Tribunal does not have any power or discretion to extend the time limit for the tenant's counter-notice. If the tenant fails to give a counter-notice in time, then the Tribunal will have no part to play, the general Notice to Quit becomes 'incontestable', and (unless it is subsequently challenged by the tenant in Court, and found to be invalid for some common law reason, e.g. for vagueness, or because it expires on the wrong day) it will bring the tenancy to an end.

There is no prescribed form which the tenant's counter-notice should take. It can be as simple as a letter, but it must make clear that the tenant proposes to rely on section 26 and wishes to refer the general notice to quit to the Tribunal.

If the tenant does give a counter-notice, in time, then the general notice to quit is not effective unless and until the landlord applies to the Tribunal (within a specified timeframe, but which can be extended by the Tribunal) and the Tribunal consents to the operation of the Notice to Quit. If the landlord does not make such an application, and/or is not in time and the Tribunal refuses to extend time, then the notice to quit is of no effect.

If seeking the Tribunal's approval of a general notice to quit, the landlord still faces two further hurdles.

The section 27 grounds

The first is that the Tribunal will only give consent if the landlord satisfies the Tribunal that one or more of the six statutory grounds for the recovery of possession applies. These are set out in section 27: (a) 'good husbandry'; (b) 'sound management of the estate'; (c) 'agricultural research or education, or for the purposes of the enactments relating to smallholdings'; (d) 'a purpose desirable for the enactments relating to allotments'; (e) 'greater hardship would be caused by withholding than by giving consent'; and (f) 'the landlord proposes to terminate the tenancy for a non-agricultural purpose'.

All these grounds have well-established meanings. However, none of these grounds is entirely straightforward for the landlord (who bears the legal and evidential burdens) to establish. Unless the landlord is taking the long shot that something will go wrong at the tenant's end so that the tenant fails to give a counter-notice in time, then the landlord must think ahead as to whether it will be able to demonstrate to the Tribunal that it genuinely meets one of the section 27 gateways.[38] If the answer to that is negative, or is in doubt, then referring the notice to the Tribunal is likely to be a waste of time and (the landlord's) money.

38 There is some recent case law which suggests that afforestation of a kind which is not ancillary to farming (and so is not agricultural within the meaning of section 96) but which does not require planning permission (and hence is not within the scope of Case B) might improve the prospects of section 27(3)(f): seek specialist advice.

The Tribunal's discretion

The second obstacle is that, even if the landlord does succeed in establishing one of the section 27 grounds, the Tribunal still has a discretion as to whether it gives its consent: the Tribunal must (not 'may') withhold consent to operation of the notice to quit if satisfied that 'in all the circumstances it appears to them that a fair and reasonable landlord would not insist on possession'. That is obviously a fact-sensitive decision. The 1986 Act does not give any further guidance, and nor do the reported cases.

It is technically possible (although in reality unlikely) that a Tribunal could consider that greater hardship would be caused to the landlord by withholding consent than to the tenant by giving consent (one of the section 27 gateways: a subjective test) but nonetheless still consider that a fair and reasonable landlord would still not insist on possession (an objective test), meaning that the Tribunal would not ultimately consent to the operation of the general Notice to Quit.

Demands for arbitration

If a notice to quit is of the kind where a challenge, under the terms of the 1986 Act, has to be referred to arbitration, and arbitration is demanded, then the notice must be referred to arbitration. The Tribunal will have no role at all.

There is no prescribed form for a demand for arbitration, but it must be in writing and must make clear that the tenant disputes the validity of the reason(s) given in the Notice to Quit, and demands arbitration.

Like a counter-notice, the tenant's demand for arbitration is also subject to a strict, non-extensible, time limit. It must be served on the landlord 'within one month' of the service of the relevant notice: The

Agricultural Holdings (Arbitration of Notices) Order 1987 SI 1987 /710 (which sets out this, and many other important, time limits for arbitration).

The following Special Cases go to the Tribunal and not to arbitration/TPD:

- Cases C and G.

The following Special Cases go to arbitration/TPD and not the Tribunal:

- Cases A, B, D, and E.

The arbitrator's powers

In relation to these latter, the arbitrator will make an award upholding or dismissing the Notice to Quit. However, an arbitral award upholding the Notice to Quit is still not an order for possession. If the tenant does not vacate, then the landlord will have to bring possession proceedings in the County Court.

If the Notice to Quit is referred to arbitration, and the tenant loses, the tenant can nonetheless still seek to challenge the validity of the Notice to Quit in court, for example by way of an arbitration appeal[39] and/or by defending possession proceedings on the ground that the Notice to Quit is vague or ambiguous.[40] Whether such rear-guard

39 If the parties to the arbitration have not agreed to exclude appeal rights, and some error of law or serious procedural irregularity giving rise to injustice can be identified: see Arbitration Act 1996 sections 67-69.

40 In *Windsor-Clive v Rees* [2021] EWHC 3180 (Ch), HHJ Jarman QC dismissed a counterclaim by the tenant (brought in response to a Case

action is sensible or worthwhile is a matter for the tenant and their advisers.

Bringing and challenging a 'Special Case' Notice to Quit

Case A: Smallholdings

There are five requirements to a successful Case A Notice to Quit, which must all be satisfied:

i. A smallholding under Agriculture Act 1970; and

ii. Let after 12th September 1984; and

iii. The tenant is over 65; and

iv. Suitable alternative living accommodation is available;[41] and

v. The tenancy agreement contains a statement that Case A shall apply.

Case A is not frequently encountered because it is available only to local authority landlords who have smallholding estates ('county farms estates') within the meaning of the Agriculture Act 1970. Although these smallholdings were intended as 'starter farms', some smallholders

---

B Notice to Quit which had been upheld at arbitration and on appeal to the High Court and which was then the basis for a claim for possession) that the tenant was, despite the valid and unappealable Notice to Quit, the beneficiary of a form of equity in the tenanted land arising from alleged representations decades earlier that he would not be required to leave the holding without 'fair compensation'.

41 This is the usual stumbling block.

did not move on to larger farms and remain in possession decades later.

The tenant's challenge to a Case A Notice to Quit begins with a 'Demand for Arbitration'. There is no prescribed form for this, but it must be in writing and must make clear that the tenant disputes the validity of the reason(s) given in the Notice to Quit, and demands arbitration. This demand must be given within one month of service of the notice to quit. If that is not done, then the Notice to Quit cannot be challenged at arbitration.

Case B: Development

The land is required for use, other than agriculture, for which actual or deemed planning permission has been granted and that fact is stated in the Notice.

Case B can be used in relation to the whole holding, or (but only in certain circumstances)[42] part of the holding.

Case B can also allow the landlord to give 'short' notice (i.e., less than the 12 months expiring on a term date which the 1986 Act otherwise requires) but only where it is given in pursuance of a provision of the contract of tenancy which authorises the resumption of possession of

---

42 Where there is a written tenancy agreement which authorises the resumption of possession of part; where part of the land is needed for the purposes set out in section 31 of the 1986 Act (eg, forestry); or where the reversion of the part required has been severed: seek specialist advice.

the holding or some part for some specified purpose other than the use of land for agriculture.[43]

If the Notice is challenged (which is by way of a demand for arbitration: see above), then it is important that the landlord can prove (albeit, in the event of dispute, only to the appropriate civil standard, ie, the balance of probabilities) that she satisfies all the elements of Case B.

There are many reported decisions on the meaning and operation of Case B Notices. Although some general principles can be stated, these are still potentially subject to challenge and argument.

What must the landlord prove?

'Required' means that the landlord must have a genuine and firm intention at the date of the notice to develop the notice land, and is not just speculating or land-banking. Except in cases where planning permission is deemed (for example under a General Development Order or an Act of Parliament), planning permission is required. However, the wording of Case B does not require full or detailed planning permission. Outline planning permission may be sufficient, even if it is subject to reserved matters.[44] A permission in outline establishes outright the principle of the proposed development and it runs with the land. Once it grants it, the planning authority cannot go back on it other than by the process of formal revocation or modification, which may entitle the developer to compensation. A subsequent approval of reserved matters does not constitute a planning

43 AHA 1986 section 25(2)(b). This obviously will not work where there is no written tenancy agreement.

44 See the discussion by Lord Gill in *The Trustees of the North Berwick Trust v James B Miller & Co* [2009] CSIH 15.

permission. It is merely an ancillary procedure by which the outline permission is made effective. The view that an outline permission suffices for the purposes of Case B also makes sense if one has regard to practice in the world of property development where, except in the case of a minor development, the making of an application in detail is rare.

Although Case B does not itself contain or express any time limit, the word 'required' may arguably (commentators differ) carry an element of timing, meaning that the landlord must be able to establish that she is able to implement the planning permission or develop at the date when the Notice expires, or within some reasonable time thereafter. But the latter – if it really is a part of the statutory test at all – is only in the sense that, if the likely commencement of the development is too far in the future, this may then cast doubt on whether the landlord really has the necessary intention to develop.

The only reported decision on the point of which I am aware is Windsor-Clive v Rees [2020] EWHC 2986 (Ch) where one of the grounds of the tenant's appeal against an arbitration award upholding a Case B Notice to Quit was an allegedly erroneous approach by the arbitrator to the words 'is required'. However, this ground of appeal had fallen away by the time of the hearing. HHJ Jarman QC, sitting as a judge of the High Court, said:

> *"The key part of Case B in the present appeal is the phrase "is required." It was ultimately not in dispute before me that that means that the land must be so required at the end of the period stated in the notice or within a relatively short time thereafter, rather than in the more distant future or at some as yet unascertained time (see Jones v Gates [1954] 1 WLR 222 at 224 [...] It is also common ground that the landlords must show an intention to develop and a reasonable prospect*

of doing so (see Paddock Investments Ltd v Lory [1975] 2 EGLR 5)."

Even if 'a reasonable time' is required, what it is will depend on the circumstances of the case, including the nature of the development. The timing of a Case B Notice to Quit (not too soon, and not too late) can therefore be an issue requiring close thought.

Other tricky issues can arise in relation to Case B: for example, whether it captures a case where a landlord seeks to recover possession for both non-agricultural and agricultural purposes,[45] or where a planning permission mandates (for example) the development of a housing estate with 'green' elements such as Sustainable Drainage Systems (SuDS) (the management of run-off water by use of rain gardens, swales, green roofs, retention ponds and soakaways etc), 'wildflower meadows' (not intended to be used for grazing, and not intended to produce a grass crop), allotment gardens, woodland etc.

More recently, questions (as yet unresolved) have arisen as to whether activities such as Biodiversity Net Gain or solar farms/PV arrays (with or without undergrazing) are 'agricultural' or not within the proper meaning and effect of Case B: seek specialist advice.

Case C: Bad husbandry

Not more than six months before the notice to quit, the Agricultural Land Tribunal granted a certificate of bad husbandry.

The recovery of possession under this Special Case is begun by the landlord applying to the Tribunal that the Tribunal should certify that

45 See the decision of the Court of Appeal in *Floyer-Acland v Osmond* [2000] 2 EGLR 1.

the tenant is not farming in accordance with the rules of good husbandry.

Those rules are set out in section 11 of the Agriculture Act 1947, and are implied into all 1986 Act tenancies.

Key amongst the rules of good husbandry is the tenant's obligation *'to maintain a reasonable standard of efficient production, as respects both the kind of produce and the quality and quantity thereof, while keeping the unit in a condition to enable such a standard to be maintained in the future...'*.

Before deciding whether to issue a certificate, the Tribunal will visit the holding so as to assess its general state and condition.

Recent emphasis on 'efficiency'

Until fairly recently, there was a widely-held view that Case C was genuinely useful only where agricultural use of the holding, or a significant part of it, had been all but abandoned.

Those were cases like Phillips v Davies (2007) which concerned 38 acres of land in Pembrokeshire. 10 acres had been abandoned, and parts of two fields had been used for dumping and burying scrap metal and other non-agricultural waste. A 2.5 acre field had a long-term dock problem. 12.5 acres/38 acres = about a third of the tenanted land. The Tribunal granted a certificate, and was upheld by the High Court on appeal: [2007] EWHC 1395 (Admin).

Another was Tarmac UK v Hughes (2009) which concerned two acres with a farmhouse which was a complete mess. Even though the management of the tenancy by the landlord had been woefully inadequate because they had not taken steps for 15 years to enforce the tenant's husbandry obligations, nonetheless, the landlord's failure had no effect on the tenant's ability to discharge his obligations of good husbandry. The Tribunal granted a certificate.

However, some – more recent – cases suggest that the approach of the Tribunal may be changing, with an increased emphasis on the long-term efficiency and economic viability of the holding, leading to certificates of bad husbandry perhaps being easier to obtain than in the past.

Treating 'efficiency' as an important word, some (albeit not all) recent cases in the Tribunal on husbandry have emphasised the underlying statutory purpose: to make sure that farms with tenants who enjoy the protection of the 1986 Act (effective lifetime security of tenure) actually keep the farm up and are farming efficiently.

In Yorke v Barron (2017) the (English) Tribunal identified serious under-stocking of a 300 acre dairy holding, with a farm business being propped up by cottage rents and horse sales. What should have been a dairy or beef producing livestock farm was neither. The farming was minimal with no discernible farming system. The horse sales were not a mere adjunct to a productive farm, but had become the core activities. The Tribunal granted a certificate of bad husbandry.

Chapman v Lumb (2015) was, to some degree, the converse. The (English) Tribunal identified serious over-stocking, with not enough cubicles, and inadequate arrangements for feed, with poor stock-management, and significant long-term disrepair and lack of maintenance. The Tribunal granted a certificate.

To my mind, the focus on efficiency and maintaining agricultural production is reflective of an overall 'direction of travel' for the 1986 Act[46], because agricultural land is a scarce and valuable resource.

However, the desire to increase "efficiency" and production is not necessarily compatible with environmental objectives and 'greening'. There may be difficult cases where the two are in conflict.

If the Tribunal grants a certificate of bad husbandry, and the landlord issues a Notice to Quit on the back of it, then the tenant's legal recourse is very limited. If intending to continue to resist possession, then the tenant can either wait for the landlord to issue possession proceedings in court, which the tenant can then defend on the basis that the notice is invalid on common law grounds, or the tenant can issue proceedings seeking a declaration that the Notice is invalid. Both these are tactics of last resort, and a tenant would have to reflect carefully as to whether the potential cost of such court proceedings (where, under the Civil Procedure Rules, costs are at large, and generally follow the event) would genuinely justify the steps taken.

Case D: Rent, and Remediable Breach of covenant

This is divided into two sub-cases.

At the date of the giving of the notice to quit, the tenant has failed to comply with either (a) a Notice to pay rent due or (b) a Notice to remedy a remediable breach.

The recovery of possession by the landlord under Case D is a notice-based system. This means that a successful Case D Notice to Quit is

46 And indeed the overall legislative apporach, post-Brexit, with its increased emphasis on domestic 'food security'.

based entirely on the tenant's failure to comply with a relevant earlier notice to pay rent due or notice to remedy a remediable breach. If the tenant has failed to comply with the relevant earlier notice, then the question of whether the rent was ever actually paid, or whether the breach was ever actually remedied, are not relevant.

Given the importance of the notices to pay rent due or remedy a remediable breach, there are very strict requirements as to the wording and service of such notices. There are statutory forms. A Notice to Pay Rent or a Notice to Remedy Breach must be in the form prescribed by the Agricultural Holdings (Notices to Pay Rent or Remedy) Regulations 1987 (SI 1987/711). That is mandatory. Hence, a failure to use the correct form will render the whole exercise invalid. The statutory forms are to be found in the Schedule to the Regulations: Form 1 is for rent; Form 2 is a notice to remedy breaches where the remedy is doing work of repair, maintenance or replacement; Form 3 is a notice to remedy breaches 'not being a notice requiring the doing of any work of repair, maintenance or replacement'.

There are important 'Act Now' and other statutorily prescribed Notes which must also be included. Punctilious compliance with the statutory forms is required.

Notices to Pay Rent

Compliance with the Notice to Pay Rent is all that really matters. If the tenant pays, but does so after the two months provided for by the standard form, then, although the rent is no longer owed, the tenant has nonetheless failed to comply with the Notice to Pay Rent, and the landlord is entitled to give a Case D Notice to Quit.[47]

47 This is the effect of the decision of the Court of Appeal in *Stoneman v*

It should be clear that any tenant who receives a Notice to Pay Rent is well-advised to comply with it, immediately, and regardless of any arguments (for example) that the tenant has already paid, or is not liable to pay because convention is that the rent is paid at the annual tenant's dinner, or because the tenant thinks he is entitled to set-off rent against a landlord's obligation to him,[48] or because the amount of rent said to be due is said to be wrongly stated.

Despite the High Court's decision in *Spencer,* it seems to me that non-compliance with a Notice to Pay Rent is a very high-risk strategy since it potentially leaves the tenant with only one line of defence against the possession proceedings which will inevitably follow, which is that the notice to pay was not valid on common law grounds (e.g., vagueness).

Other Case D Notices

Remediable breaches are breaches of covenants which are regarded (as a matter of law) as capable of being remedied. Frequently-encountered examples include breaches of covenants to reside in the farmhouse, or to use the farmhouse as a private dwelling only (this could, for example, technically be broken if the tenant used part of the

---

Brown [1973] 1 WLR 459. There was no defence to the claim for possession.

48 Although in *Secretary of State for Defence v Spencer* [2019] EWHC 1526 (Ch), the High Court (on appeal) held that a 1986 Act tenant could resist a Case D notice to pay, on the basis that it overstated the rent due, because of an equitable set-off of an unliquidated claim for damages, but only so long as the set-off was 'properly asserted' and 'quantified' 'reasonably and in good faith'.

farmhouse as the farm office). Irremediable breaches are dealt with under Case E: see below.

A Notice to Do Works (Form 2) and A Notice to Remedy Breach not doing works (Form 3) each give notice to remedy the alleged breach within a period set down by the landlord.

A challenge to a Notice to Do Works (Form 2) is by way of a demand for arbitration, in the one-month timescale, followed by an arbitration (for example, on whether there is any breach, and, if there is, the length of time given to remedy it).[49]

The 1986 Act gives the tenant a lifeline: even if a Notice to Quit based on the tenant's failure to comply with a Form 2 notice is upheld at arbitration, the tenant may still (within one month after the award) give a counter-notice invoking the Tribunal's jurisdiction. The landlord must then apply to the Tribunal for consent to the operation of his notice to quit. The Tribunal must consent unless it appears to them, having regard to the extent to which the tenant has failed to comply with the notice to do work, the consequences of his failure to comply with the notice in any respect, and the circumstances surrounding any such failure, that a fair and reasonable landlord would not insist on possession: AHA 1986 section 28(5).

Neither a Form 1 (Notice to Pay) or a Form 3 (notice to remedy breach not doing works) can be referred to arbitration until a later notice to quit is served on the ground that the tenant failed to comply with an earlier Notice to Pay or Form 3 notice.

49 Both might throw up difficult factual and legal issues.

Unlike Form 2, if the tenant fails to successfully challenge a Notice to Quit based on a Form 3 notice to remedy at arbitration, there is no role for the Tribunal.

Case E: Irremediable Breach

At the date of the notice, the landlord's interest has been materially prejudiced by an irremediable breach of any term or condition of the tenancy agreement, by the tenant, which is not inconsistent with the tenant's duty to farm in accordance with the rules of good husbandry.

Irremediable breaches are breaches of covenants which are regarded – as a matter of law – as incapable of being remedied. These are less common than remediable breaches, which are dealt with under Case D. The most frequently-encountered example of an irremediable breach is an assignment or sub-letting in breach of covenant.[50]

The landlord must be able to demonstrate that the landlord's interest has been *"materially prejudiced"* by the breach. This is undefined, but a sound approach is that the breach has got to have a material adverse impact on the reversion. What is 'material' may depend on the circumstances of the case. Moreover, the breach which is alleged to have taken place should be "not inconsistent" with the tenant's duties in respect of good husbandry (see above).

Challenge to a Case E Notice is by way of a demand for arbitration, in the one-month timescale, followed by an arbitration.

50 The assignment, even if in breach of covenant, is nonetheless effective to convey the legal estate.

Case F: Insolvency

The tenant has become insolvent.

'Insolvent' is defined in section 96(2) of the 1986 Act. For an individual, it means adjudged bankrupt, or entered into an Individual Voluntary Agreement. For a corporate body, it means wound-up or subject to a resolution to wind up. There are obvious gaps in the legislation (not least insofar as it fails to make mention of the Insolvency Act 1986).

This potentially offers a relatively quick and straightforward way of recovering possession. However, the change in the 'bankruptcy limit' (increased in 2015 from £750 to £5000) has inevitably discouraged landlords from issuing a Statutory Demand (which, if not met, could then be used as a springboard to petition for the tenant's bankruptcy) unless they are owed more than £5,000.

Of course, rent owing of less than £5,000 – even £1 – is still capable of being the subject of a Notice to Pay Rent which, if not complied with within the two months allowed, will found an incontestable Case D Notice to Quit.

But, if available, Case F is nonetheless very useful to the landlord because the general rule in section 25 that a notice to quit an agricultural holding has to give at least 12 months expiring on the term date does <u>not</u> apply where the tenant is insolvent (s.25(2)(a)), meaning that the landlord can give shorter notice.

Any challenge to a Case F notice has to be in court, either by way of defending the landlord's claim to possession, or bringing a claim for a declaration that the Case F notice is invalid, but bearing in mind the comments above – see Case C – as to the advisability of such a course of action.

Case G: Tenant's death

The tenant has died and less than three months has passed since the landlord received relevant notice.

The tenant's death does not bring the tenancy to an end. It vests in the personal representatives.

'The relevant notice' to the landlord referred to in Case G can be either written notice from the personal representatives (for which there is no prescribed form) or service on the landlord of an application for a succession tenancy (which must be made within three months of the tenant's death).

In the absence of such 'relevant notice', time will not begin to run against the landlord for the purposes of the landlord's Case G notice, even if he happens to know of the tenant's death (for example, if he carried the tenant's coffin at the funeral).[51]

In the case of an intestate tenant, written notice has to come from the personal representatives. Therefore, it cannot be given before letters of administration have been obtained.

If the tenant died testate, the personal representatives derive their authority from the will and notification to the landlord at any time after the death by those persons will start time running.

If a succession application is made, then the landlord applies to the Tribunal for consent to the operation of a Case G notice to quit.

51 See, for example, *Lees v Tatchell* [1990] 1 EGLR 10

Case H: Minister's certificate

Restructuring or reshaping of agricultural units.

This Special Case is only available to the Secretary of State. You are unlikely to encounter one (I never have). If you do, consult one of the standard practitioners' works, or seek specialist advice.

CHAPTER FOUR

SUCCESSION TO A 1986 ACT TENANCY

Succession is a very important feature of some tenancies under the 1986 Act. But rights to apply to succeed to an AHT generally exist only where (i) the tenancy was first granted before 12th July 1984, or (ii) if the tenancy was first granted between 12 July 1984 and 1 September 1995, the parties expressly contracted into the succession provisions of the 1986 Act, or (iii) the tenancy itself is a (first) successor tenancy.

Succession rights are potentially exercisable on up to two occasions, on the tenant's death or retirement. The provisions relating to succession on death and on retirement are broadly similar.

Succession applications to the Tribunal on the death of the tenant

The aspirant successor must make an application to the Tribunal within 3 months of the date of death. **Time is of the essence.** The 3-month deadline is strict and cannot be extended by the Tribunal. For that reason, it is wise to try to avoid last-minute applications, even if doing so is tempting because (for example) there are discussions between the prospective successor and the landlord. The fact of ongoing discussions, no matter how cordial and productive, does not exempt the applicant from applying to the Tribunal in time. If the applicant does not apply within three months, and negotiations break down, then the applicant is left in real jeopardy.

Use the appropriate Tribunal form (available online) but note that the Tribunal in England and the Tribunal in Wales use different forms. Notice should also be given to the landlord (not least, because the making of an application to succeed starts the landlord's clock running to give a Case G Notice to Quit). The aspirant successor should attach as much supporting information to the form as she can. But the most important thing is to file the application form on time. That should not be put on hold whilst supporting paperwork is assembled. With the Tribunal's permission, that can be provided later.

If the landlord wishes to oppose the application, or comment on it, she must complete and return to the Tribunal the appropriate form within the timescale set down by the Rules.

The landlord can also resist a succession application by issuing a Case G notice, and then applying to the Tribunal for consent to its operation. If this happens, then the Tribunal will (usually) first determine the application to succeed before going on to determine whether the landlord's Case G notice should have effect.

The two questions: 'eligibility' and 'suitability'

An aspirant successor must prove to the Tribunal that she is both 'eligible' and 'suitable'.

Both concepts can present difficulties for applicants. The 1986 Act is now perhaps showing its age. The legislation was better suited to a model of farms and farming where the farm was economically self-sufficient – in the sense that the farm income was both sufficient to support the farming family (without the need for anyone to work elsewhere) and came entirely from the production of food (and not from activities off the farm, or diversified activities on the farm). These remarks are especially relevant when it comes to consider whether the applicant satisfies the 'livelihood' condition, which is an element of eligibility.

Eligibility

Eligibility is technical, and can be arbitrary.

Close relative

The applicant must be a 'close relative' of the deceased tenant. This is defined by the 1986 Act (as amended) as meaning a spouse or civil partner, a sibling, a child (including step or adopted children) or "any person (not being a sibling or a child) who, in the case of any marriage or civil partnership to which the deceased was at any time a party, was treated by the deceased as a child of the family in relation to that marriage or civil partnership."

There are obvious omissions from this list, such as grandchildren, nephews, and nieces. They are not 'close relatives', as defined, and therefore are not eligible to apply to succeed and cannot do so. The Tribunal has no power or discretion to consider an application by someone who is not a close relative. If such a person wishes to take a tenancy, then they will have to try to negotiate a solution with the landlord.

There are other anomalies. For example, where two siblings (one with children, one childless) hold the tenancy as joint tenants, and survivorship operates, whether any of the children can apply to succeed on the death or retirement of the surviving joint tenant depends on which sibling dies first. If the sibling with children dies first, the tenancy survives to the unmarried sibling, and the nieces and nephews are not his close relatives and cannot apply. If the childless sibling dies first, then the tenancy survives to the parent sibling, and the children are eligible to apply. The scenario is so common as to be popularly (but inaccurately) known as 'the bachelor trap'.

The 'livelihood condition'

The second part of eligibility is the livelihood condition.

The Applicant must satisfy the Tribunal that '*in the seven years ending with the date of death*' (of the former tenant) the applicant's '*only or principal source of livelihood throughout a continuous period of not less than five years, or two or more discontinuous period together amounting to not less than five years, derived from his agricultural work on the holding or on an agricultural unit of which the holding forms part*': AHA 1986 section 36(3)(a)

This is often the main battleground in disputed applications by a close relative to succeed to the tenancy.

There are several issues to consider. The first is the proper meaning of 'agricultural work'. Manual work on the farm (milking etc) should straightforwardly qualify. Qualifying work probably includes work which is closely connected with the agricultural activity on the holding, but which is not actually done on the farm, such as agricultural contracting (using the farm's equipment to cut hedges etc for other farmers) or cattle-dealing. It may also catch work which contributes to the agricultural activity but which is 'white collar' rather than muddy boots (for instance, keeping the farm's books and records).

More challenging scenarios can arise where the applicant has worked on the farm, but this work has been part of a diversified enterprise such as running a farm shop, or a B&B in the farmhouse. Such work does not (at least on the face of it) fall squarely within the definition of 'agriculture' given in section 96 of the Act, which has to be met if the tenancy is to be the tenancy of an *agricultural* holding. Whilst some legislative tinkering in 2006[52] allowed such work to qualify for the purposes of the livelihood condition if the landlord had approved of it in writing, there is no compulsion on a landlord to do so, and it is not obvious why (except for philanthropy) a landlord would want to do so voluntarily.

'Principal' just means 'more than half': 50.01% would be good enough. 49.99% would not be good enough.

'Livelihood' can prove to be a difficult and controversial issue. In the leading case, Caswell v Welby [1995] 71 P & CR 137, the Court of Appeal said that livelihood was to be defined as *'means of living, that is to say what is spent or consumed for the purpose of living. The source of one's livelihood insofar as it is money is income; insofar as it is the use or consumption of goods, it is benefits in kind'.*

An applicant may have income derived from one or more sources. If so, in order to qualify, the income derived from work on the agricultural holding must be greater than the income from other sources.

The Court of Appeal was clear that section 36(3)(a) was to be construed in a purposive and common-sense way, as a jury would do, and without adopting too legalistic an approach. The section simply requires the Applicant to establish their economic dependence on the holding by showing that their work on the holding provided their main means of livelihood.

52 *The Regulatory Reform (Agricultural Tenancies) (England and Wales) Order 2006*, SI 2006/2805

The Tribunal is an adversarial jurisdiction, and the Applicant's task of discharging their burden on the livelihood issue is ordinarily gone about by putting forward a sufficient body of evidence which can be assessed (in the first instance) by the Respondent to decide whether it continues to oppose the application in whole or in part; and, after that, if the application remains in dispute, which can be assessed and tested by the Tribunal. Meaningful assessment can only be done with adequate evidence. Without adequate evidence, an Applicant will struggle to meet their burden on eligibility, and in consequence their application would fail.

Despite the Court of Appeal's guidance, and reticence sometimes expressed by the Tribunal in dealing with disclosure applications,[53] parties nonetheless do sometimes spend a lot of time, effort, and money in a forensic dissection of the applicant's livelihood, in the attempt either (on the part of the applicant) to reach a figure of over 50% (even marginally) for 5 of 7 years, or (on the part of the landlord) to drive the figure down to less (even marginally) than 50% for 3 of 7 years.

The Tribunal has itself also, on occasion, been tempted by such efforts, engaging in complex calculations (for example) as to the value of the applicant's bed and board in the farmhouse as opposed to living and eating elsewhere. But parties should reflect on whether such detailed effort genuinely reflects the guidance of the Court of Appeal, and/or whether it is genuinely justified in cases where livelihood, one way or the other, and even on a broad-brush basis, seems fairly clear.

53 See, for example, the decisions of the Wales Tribunal in *Silverthorne v Bowen* (ALT12/2020, May 2025) and *Lewis v Ceredigion County Council* (ALT 02/2025 and ALT 03/2025, August 2025) where the Tribunal rejected wide-ranging disclosure orders sought by landlords; and requirements that there be expert evidence.

Further complexity is potentially introduced by the issue of resources other than the applicant's. On one view, this is irrelevant: the livelihood test, as set out in the statute, applies only to the applicant for succession, and to no-one else. When it comes to the income of an applicant's spouse or civil partner, it is to be noted that section 36(3)(a) is not an *income* test, let alone a 'joint income' test. Caswell v Welby itself touches on some of these issues, but it cannot be said for sure that questions as to whether the income or livelihood of an applicant's spouse or civil partner, or the generosity or benevolence of relatives, are always irrelevant.

Section 41: 'material extent' and fairness

Here, but only in the event of applications to succeed on the *death* of the tenant (and not in the event of applications to succeed on the tenant's retirement) section 41 of the 1986 Act provides an important degree of latitude when it comes to assessing the applicant's livelihood. Where an applicant is otherwise, and in all respects, an eligible person, but the source of livelihood test, although not fully satisfied, is satisfied to "a material extent", and it would be fair and reasonable to treat him or her as fully eligible, then the applicant can apply to be treated as fully eligible.

This has to be specifically applied for on the application form. If it is not so applied for, the Tribunal may not be able to consider it. So, and even if you are sure that you will comfortably satisfy the livelihood condition, tick the box!

What is 'a material extent' is a matter of fact and degree. This may depend on whether the failure to meet the livelihood condition was a 'near' miss or not, both in terms of years, and in terms of percentage.

The uncertainty of approach is to some degree illustrated by *Holder v Woods*.[54] There, the Tribunal held that 6 years (out of 7) of livelihood under 51% did not satisfy the material extent test; but also held that the test would have been met had there been 3 years over 50%.[55]

The statute gives no further guidance as to what is 'fair and reasonable'. This has to be a matter of fact and degree.

Not an occupier of a commercial unit.

Until reforms introduced by the *Agriculture Act 2020* came into force in 2024, there was a third element of eligibility which had to be satisfied. This has now been abolished, but mention is made of it just for the sake of completeness.

This (now abolished) third element was that the applicant could not themselves be in occupation of a commercial unit of agricultural land: section 36(3)(b). The gist of this condition – perhaps reflecting an old-fashioned notion of dynastic farming, with prospective successors staying to work on the farm rather than spreading their wings and going elsewhere – was that a successor had to be economically dependent on their work on the subject holding; and, if they already occupied a suitably sized holding elsewhere, capable of supporting them economically, then they would be expected to make their living from that.

Fortunately, the complex rules of what amounted to occupation, and the need to conduct a 'Net Annual Income Assessment' are now

---

54 ALD/SW/S/2021/006 (November 2025)

55 This in turn depended on whether the income coming from agricultural work on the holding and on another unit (not part of the holding) were to be split 70:30 or 80:20 – a fine distinction indeed.

abolished, and it is very unlikely that anyone reading this edition will be contending with a pre-2024 succession application where the issue of commercial occupation has not already been addressed.

Suitability

Having dealt with eligibility, the Tribunal must also be satisfied that the applicant is, 'in their opinion', 'a suitable person to become the tenant of the holding'. The suitability test is free-standing from eligibility, meaning that an *eligible* applicant may nonetheless not be *suitable* to become tenant.

The new test

In assessing suitability, section 39(8A) of the 1986 Act (amended by the *Agriculture Act 2020*) now sets down a two-stage test.

The first stage is that the Tribunal is to have regard to 'all relevant matters (including the landlord's views as to suitability) including:

(a) the person's likely capability and capacity to farm the holding commercially, with or without other land, taking into account the need for high standards of efficient production and care for the environment in relation to managing that holding;

(b) the person's experience, training and skills in agriculture and business management;

(c) the person's financial standing and their character;

(d) the character, situation and condition of the holding; and

(e) the terms of the tenancy.

The second stage is that, 'having had regard to all relevant matters', 'the Tribunal must be satisfied that, if the applicant had applied in an open competition for a tenancy of this holding, that is assumed to be available under the 1986 Act, a prudent and willing landlord could reasonably be expected to regard the applicant as among the candidates to whom they would be willing to grant the tenancy.'

The Tribunal must disregard (a) all offers as to rent in relation to the holding; and (b) the age of the person applying.

The legal and evidential burden of satisfying the Tribunal is on the Applicant, who must collect and put forward sufficient evidence to satisfy the Tribunal that the Applicant is suitable. This may well have practical implications in terms of the sort of evidence to be assembled and presented: for example, whether this includes things like business plans, budgets, and/or demonstrable access to finance.

It is to be noted that the statutory factors are not exhaustive. Something sometimes encountered is an applicant who has criminal convictions. These may be potentially relevant (for example, disqualification from driving on the public roads may affect an applicant's ability to get from one part of the holding to another) although the Act is careful to describe the test as one of suitability and not one of moral character.

The Tribunal has a wide discretion. Here, it has to be borne in mind that the Tribunal is usually made up of a panel of three people – a legally qualified chair, sitting with a farmer and a landowner.

If an applicant satisfies the Tribunal that she is both eligible and suitable, then (unless the landlord has served a Case G Special Case Notice, and can gain the Tribunal's to its operation) the Tribunal must make a direction entitling the applicant to the grant of a new tenancy, the terms of which will be the same as the terms of the old tenancy.

Succession applications to the Tribunal on the retirement of the tenant

These are less frequently encountered than applications to succeed on death. Such applications are potentially deterred by two quirks of the rules.

The first quirk is that section 41 of the 1986 Act does not apply to applications to succeed on retirement. Therefore, in retirement cases, the applicant has to satisfy the livelihood condition: there is no 'material extent' fall-back.

The second quirk is that an unsuccessful application for succession on retirement bars the same person from later applying to succeed on the tenant's death.[56]

The rules as to eligibility and suitability are otherwise the same as for applications to succeed on death.

The tenant has to give a retirement notice. The requirement that the tenant must have reached the age of 65 at the date the retirement notice takes effect has now been abolished. There is no longer a minimum retirement age.

The retirement notice has to take effect on the term date at least 12 months from the date of the notice. It must contain the nomination

56 AHA 1986, section 53

of one person, eligible within the meaning of the Act, as successor. It is not possible to nominate more than one person.

CHAPTER FIVE

DISPUTE RESOLUTION

The Resolution of Disputes outside the Tribunal

Arbitration of FBTs

In relation to FBTs under the 1995 Act, section 28 provides that any dispute between the landlord and tenant under an FBT concerning their rights and obligations under the 1995 Act, 'shall be determined by arbitration'. However, there are exceptions. Section 29 provides that an FBT can contain its own dispute resolution mechanism, therefore overriding section 28.

Arbitration of AHTs

The 1986 Act provides that many matters of dispute have to be referred to arbitration. Some have been discussed above – for example, Schedule 1 matters, and certain sorts of Special Case Notices to Quit. There are others, such as compensation for fixed equipment, rent review, and settlement of certain claims at the end of the tenancy.

Arbitrations generally are governed by the detailed rules of the *Arbitration Act 1996*. Section 1 sets out the object of arbitration, which is to obtain the fair resolution of disputes by an impartial tribunal without unnecessary delay or expense, adopting procedures (for example, about evidence, documents, and submissions) which are suitable to the circumstances of the particular case. Section 34 sets out the arbitrator's general case-management powers.

Despite these aims, it should not be assumed that arbitration is invariably a quick and straightforward way of resolving the dispute, or even that it will be quicker and more straightforward than going to court.

The costs of arbitration

An important matter to be considered before embarking on arbitration are the potential costs, and the potential incidence of those costs. Arbitrations can be (very) expensive. In contrast to court proceedings, where the judge is paid for through general taxation, the arbitrator will charge the parties a professional fee for their services. Non-lawyer arbitrators sometimes appoint legal advisers or assessors to advise the arbitrator as to legal aspects of the dispute, and this adviser/assessor will also be entitled to charge a professional fee for their services.

The arbitrator may make an award allocating the costs of the arbitration – which are the arbitrator's fees and expenses, the fees and expenses of any arbitral institution concerned, and the legal or other costs of the parties – as between the parties. Unless the parties otherwise agree, the arbitrator shall award costs on the general principle that costs should follow the event except where it appears to the arbitrator that in the circumstances it is not appropriate in relation to the whole or part of the costs: section 61 of the Arbitration Act 1996.

The second aspect is complexity. Except for location and the absence of wigs and gowns, arbitrations can sometimes be indistinguishable from a fully-fledged conventional court case, with witnesses giving oral evidence, and that oral evidence being tested by way of cross-examination.

Third Party Determination

These factors gave rise to significant and well-publicised criticism of the general operation of the Arbitration Act. In response to this, Schedule 4 of Deregulation Act 2015 now provides that certain disputes can be resolved by 'third party determination' rather than by arbitration. Third party determination is therefore a possibility, but the rules and governing principles are unclear, and seem to be largely (if not entirely) in the hands of the parties.

The third party must be appointed in writing. It is obvious that great care will have to be taken in drafting such an agreement, since the relationship between the parties and the third party, the third party's obligations, and the circumstances in which the decision will be final and/or binding on the parties will need to be governed by the terms of the contract. It would be most unfortunate if the parties, having appointed a third party, then had to go to Court to elicit the meaning of their agreement. Unlike arbitration, the procedure to be adopted is not automatically governed by statute. Hence, unless the parties seek to adopt and incorporate, 'off-the-peg', a ready-made code (such as, for example, the Arbitration Act) then they are thrown to their own resources.

Third Party Determination is very different to arbitration. It is subject to very little review or intervention by the court. The third party is not a judge, and is not performing a judicial function. The process (whatever the parties agree it should be) leads to a 'determination', and not to an award or a judgment. Unless the parties agree otherwise, there is no right of appeal.

It is not entirely clear whether a determination could be impeached – for instance, if the third party arrived at a determination on a fundamentally erroneous and demonstrable factual basis. The most careful approach would be to expressly provide for the grounds of challenge in the TPD contract: e.g., departure from instructions; exceeding the agreed ambit of the determination; or manifest error of fact (or, perhaps, error of law).

Dispute Resolution in the Tribunal

The following remarks are intended to be general guidance to those who need to deal with the Tribunals.

Forms:

1. Use the Tribunal's website to find out whether there is a particular form which should be used (there usually will be).

2. If a form is in PDF format, and you do not have a programme which allows you to fill it in, ask the Tribunal if it has a form in Word or some other editable format.

3. If the Tribunal does not have a form in a format which you can complete on a computer, print off the form, complete it by hand, and scan it and email it back. Do not trust to the post.

4. If putting a form in the post, copy or take a photo of the whole form for your records. Do not rely on the Tribunal later being able to supply you with copies of what you have sent.

5. If time is of the essence (it often is) then use recorded delivery and/or get a certificate of posting to avoid disputes about timing.

Writing to the Tribunal:

6. The Tribunal manages a caseload. Whenever you correspond with the Tribunal, put the case details (eg names, and land) and number (if you have one) clearly at the top of your email or letter.

7. Always identify on whose behalf you are writing (eg, 'I am the Applicant', or 'I am the Applicant's solicitor'). Do not leave the Tribunal to have to work it out.

8. Whenever you write, copy your letter to the other party(ies), and make it clear on your letter or email that you have done so (eg, 'I am copying this email to all the other parties: you will see their email addresses are in the copy to box above). The Tribunal has to deal openly and transparently with the parties, and cannot correspond with one party without being confident that all parties are seeing the correspondence.

9. The Tribunal's staff are civil servants and are entitled to respect in the workplace. Be courteous in all your dealings with them.

10. Write only when you really have a good purpose. Write in terms which are as simple and straightforward as you can. Know what you are asking for, and why. Do not leave the Tribunal to have to try to puzzle it out.

Your case:

11. The Tribunal is an independent judicial body and cannot give you legal advice.

12. If the Tribunal writes to you with directions for the management of your case, the directions are orders, and not suggestions, and must be complied with.

13. If you cannot comply with a direction in time, contact the Tribunal, preferably in advance of the date, explain the situation, and ask for more time. Open-ended requests for more time are less likely to be favourably received than those which set out a realistic timescale.

14. The Tribunal's letters, if dealing with a substantive matter, and even if signed by a Tribunal official, are often drafted by a judge, and may contain valuable guidance as to further steps.

Hearings:

15. The Tribunal's hearings are normally held in public, and not in private.

16. Expect a panel of three – a legally-qualified chairperson and two (usually, not legally qualified) 'wingers' – usually a 'farmer' member and a 'landowner' member.

17. Site visits and inspections are an important fact-finding part of many of the Tribunal's cases (and are, formally, a part of the hearing).

18. The Tribunal is an adversarial jurisdiction: it decides the cases which are brought to it and answers the questions which it is asked to answer. The evidence which the parties choose to advance is, by and large, a matter of choice for the parties, albeit subject to control by the Tribunal. The Tribunal is not an inquisitorial jurisdiction and does not have a mandate to engage in detective work.

APPENDIX A

SUGGESTED FURTHER READING

Halsbury's Laws of England, Volume 1 – 'Agricultural Law and Allotments'.

Muir Watt and Moss, 'Agricultural Holdings' (16th edition, 2024, ed Sir T Fancourt and others)

Christopher Rodgers and Nerys Llewellyn Jones, Agricultural Law (5th edition forthcoming, March 2026)

Scammell Densham and Williams (ed PR Williams) 'The Law of Agricultural Holdings' (11th edition, 2023)

APPENDIX B

USEFUL ADDRESSES AND CONTACT DETAILS

Agricultural Land Tribunal for Wales

Agricultural Land Tribunal Wales
Welsh Tribunals Unit
PO Box 100
Llandrindod Wells
Powys
LD1 9BW
http://agriculturallandtribunal.gov.wales
Email: agriculturallandtribunal@gov.wales
Phone: 0300 025 9809

Agricultural Land Tribunal for England

First-tier Tribunal (Property Chamber)
Agricultural Land and Drainage
1st Floor, Piccadilly Exchange
Piccadilly Plaza
Manchester
M1 4AH
Email: aldgeneralenquiries@justice.gov.uk
Phone: 0161 237 9491
Fax: 01264 785 128

Agricultural Law Association Dispute Resolution Panel

aladisputeresolution.co.uk

Office 1
The Stackyard
Bulwick
Northamptonshire
NN17 3DY
http://ala.org.uk
Email: enquiries@ala.org.

MORE BOOKS BY LAW BRIEF PUBLISHING

A selection of our other titles available now:-

'A Practical Guide to Probation Breaches and Other Applications' by Mark Thomas
'A Practical Guide to Remarriage and Divorce' by Cordelia Williams & Claire Howard
'A Practical Guide to Privacy, Transparency, Reporting Restrictions and Closed Proceedings in the Court of Protection' by Laura Mannering
'Beaumont on Barristers – A Guide to Defending Disciplinary Proceedings (Second Edition)' by Marc Beaumont
'A Practical Guide to Payments for Environmental Services' by Ben Sharples
'A Practical Guide to the Law of Pregnancy and Maternity at Work' by Rebecca Thomas
'A Practical Guide to Redundancy – Second Edition' by Philip Hyland & Collette Moore
'A Practical Guide to International Issues for Scottish Family Lawyers' by Susie Mountain, Donna McKay, Ken MacDonald
'A Practical Guide to the Law on Deprivation of Liberty' by Ben Troke
'A Practical Guide to Rights over Airspace and Subsoil – Second Edition' by Daniel Gatty
'A Practical Guide to the Law in Relation to Inquests' by Ramya Nagesh
'A Practical Guide to the Construction and Rectification of Wills and Trust Instruments (Second Edition)' by Edward Hewitt
'A Practical Guide to Data Protection in Social Housing' by Clare Paterson
'A Practical Guide to Spousal Maintenance – Second Edition' by Liz Cowell
'A Practical Guide to International Parental Child Abduction Law (England and Wales)' by Dr Onyója Momoh
'A Practical Guide to Deprivation of British Citizenship' by Sean Ell
'A Practical Guide to Commercial Property Service Charges' by Rachel Garton
'A Practical Guide to Clinical Negligence – Third Edition' by Geoffrey Simpson-Scott (Geoff)
'A Practical Guide to the Rights of Grandparents in Children Proceedings – Second Edition' by Stuart Barlow

'The Electronic Communications Code: A Practical Guide – Second Edition' by Kerry Bretherton KC, James Castle, Mark Loveday
'A Practical Guide to the Independent School Standards – September 2023 Edition' by Sarah McKimm
'A Practical Guide to Estate Administration and Crypto Assets' by Richard Marshall
'A Practical Guide to Parental Alienation in Private and Public Law Children Cases' by Sam King QC & Frankie Shama
'Contested Heritage – Removing Art from Land and Historic Buildings' by Richard Harwood QC, Catherine Dobson, David Sawtell
'The Limits of Separate Legal Personality: When Those Running a Company Can Be Held Personally Liable for Losses Caused to Third Parties Outside of the Company' by Dr Mike Wilkinson
'A Practical Guide to Transgender Law' by Robin Moira White & Nicola Newbegin
'A Practical Guide to 'Stranded Spouses' in Family Law' by Mani Singh Basi
'A Practical Guide to Residential Freehold Conveyancing' by Lorraine Richardson
'A Practical Guide to Pensions on Divorce for Lawyers' by Bryan Scant
'A Practical Guide to Challenging Sham Marriage Allegations in Immigration Law' by Priya Solanki
'A Practical Guide to Digital Communications Evidence in Criminal Law' by Sam Willis
'A Practical Guide to Legal Rights in Scotland' by Sarah-Jane Macdonald
'A Practical Guide to New Build Conveyancing' by Paul Sams & Rebecca East
'A Practical Guide to Inherited Wealth on Divorce' by Hayley Trim
'A Practical Guide to Practice Direction 12J and Domestic Abuse in Private Law Children Proceedings' by Rebecca Cross & Malvika Jaganmohan
'A Practical Guide to Confiscation and Restraint' by Narita Bahra QC, John Carl Townsend, David Winch
'A Practical Guide to the Law of Forests in Scotland' by Philip Buchan
'A Practical Guide to Health and Medical Cases in Immigration Law' by Rebecca Chapman & Miranda Butler
'A Practical Guide to Bad Character Evidence for Criminal Practitioners by Aparna Rao
'A Practical Guide to Extradition Law post-Brexit' by Myles Grandison et al
'A Practical Guide to Hoarding and Mental Health for Housing Lawyers' by Rachel Coyle

‘Stephens on Contractual Indemnities’ by Richard Stephens

‘A Practical Guide to the EU Succession Regulation’ by Richard Frimston

‘A Practical Guide to Solicitor and Client Costs – Second Edition’ by Robin Dunne

‘Constructive Dismissal – Practice Pointers and Principles’ by Benjimin Burgher

‘A Practical Guide to Religion and Belief Discrimination Claims in the Workplace’ by Kashif Ali

‘A Practical Guide to the Law of Medical Treatment Decisions’ by Ben Troke

‘Fundamental Dishonesty and QOCS in Personal Injury Proceedings: Law and Practice’ by Jake Rowley

‘A Practical Guide to the Law in Relation to School Exclusions’ by Charlotte Hadfield & Alice de Coverley

‘A Practical Guide to Divorce for the Silver Separators’ by Karin Walker

‘The Right to be Forgotten – The Law and Practical Issues’ by Melissa Stock

‘A Practical Guide to Planning Law and Rights of Way in National Parks, the Broads and AONBs’ by James Maurici QC, James Neill et al

‘A Practical Guide to Election Law’ by Tom Tabori

‘A Practical Guide to the Law in Relation to Surrogacy’ by Andrew Powell

‘A Practical Guide to Claims Arising from Fatal Accidents – Second Edition’ by James Patience

‘A Practical Guide to Asbestos Claims’ by Jonathan Owen & Gareth McAloon

‘A Practical Guide to Stamp Duty Land Tax in England and Northern Ireland’ by Suzanne O’Hara

‘A Practical Guide to the Law of Farming Partnerships’ by Philip Whitcomb

‘A Practical Guide to the Law of Unlawful Eviction and Harassment – Second Edition’ by Stephanie Lovegrove

‘A Practical Guide to Costs in Personal Injury Claims – Second Edition’ by Matthew Hoe

‘A Practical Guide to the General Data Protection Regulation (GDPR) – Second Edition’ by Keith Markham

‘A Practical Guide to Working with Litigants in Person and McKenzie Friends in Family Cases’ by Stuart Barlow

‘Protecting Unregistered Brands: A Practical Guide to the Law of Passing Off’ by Lorna Brazell

‘A Practical Guide to Secondary Liability and Joint Enterprise Post-Jogee’ by Joanne Cecil & James Mehigan

'A Practical Guide to the Pre-Action RTA Claims Protocol for Personal Injury Lawyers' by Antonia Ford
'A Practical Guide to Neighbour Disputes and the Law' by Alexander Walsh
'A Practical Guide to Coercive Control for Legal Practitioners and Victims' by Rachel Horman
'A Practical Guide to the Law of Driverless Cars – Second Edition'
by Alex Glassbrook, Emma Northey & Scarlett Milligan
'A Practical Guide to TOLATA Claims' by Greg Williams
'A Practical Guide to Elderly Law – Second Edition' by Justin Patten
'A Practical Guide to Responding to Housing Disrepair and Unfitness Claims' by Iain Wightwick
'A Practical Guide to the Law of Bullying and Harassment in the Workplace' by Philip Hyland
'How to Be a Freelance Solicitor: A Practical Guide to the SRA-Regulated Freelance Solicitor Model' by Paul Bennett
'A Practical Guide to Prison Injury Claims' by Malcolm Johnson
'A Practical Guide to Advising Clients at the Police Station' by Colin Stephen McKeown-Beaumont
'A Practical Guide to Antisocial Behaviour Injunctions – Second Edition' by Iain Wightwick
'Practical Mediation: A Guide for Mediators, Advocates, Advisers, Lawyers, and Students in Civil, Commercial, Business, Property, Workplace, and Employment Cases' by Jonathan Dingle with John Sephton
'The Mini-Pupillage Workbook' by David Boyle
'A Practical Guide to Crofting Law' by Brian Inkster
'A Practical Guide to the Law of Domain Names and Cybersquatting' by Andrew Clemson
'A Practical Guide to the Law of Gender Pay Gap Reporting' by Harini Iyengar
'NHS Whistleblowing and the Law' by Joseph England
'Employment Law and the Gig Economy' by Nigel Mackay & Annie Powell
'A Practical Guide to Noise Induced Hearing Loss (NIHL) Claims' by Andrew Mckie, Ian Skeate, Gareth McAloon
'An Introduction to Beauty Negligence Claims – A Practical Guide for the Personal Injury Practitioner' by Greg Almond
'Intercompany Agreements for Transfer Pricing Compliance' by Paul Sutton
'Zen and the Art of Mediation' by Martin Plowman
'A Practical Guide to Adoption for Family Lawyers' by Graham Pegg

www.ingramcontent.com/pod-product-compliance
Lightning Source LLC
LaVergne TN
LVHW022310200926
848481LV00004B/1275
* 9 7 8 1 9 1 8 2 4 1 3 6 5 *